GOSPEL IN
THE LION KING

By
SIMBARASHE
CHARUMBIRA

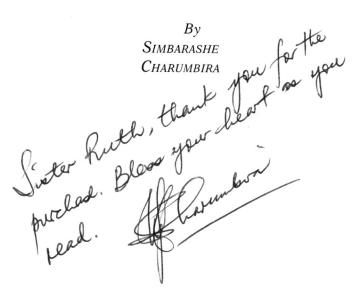

TEACH Services, Inc.
Brushton, New York

2010 11 12 13 14 · 5 4 3 2 1

Copyright © 2010 Simbarashe Charumbria and
TEACH Services, Inc.
ISBN-13: 978-1-57258-560-7
Library of Congress Control Number: 2010921366

Published by

TEACH Services, Inc.
www.TEACHServices.com

TABLE OF CONTENTS

ACKNOWLEDGMENTS

This book is dedicated to my dear parents Job and Margaret Charumbira who worked diligently to raise a young boy to love the Lord. Many thanks to my two brothers Job and Isheanesu, and my sister and her husband Shupikai and Tinashe Makumbe for your unwavering support. I love you pricelessly.

Special thanks to Jeanette Bryson for reading and editing the original manuscript.

Dr. Pardon Mwansa, your Hebrew and Greek classes had a positive influence on my understanding of the gospel; thanks for reading my manuscript and offering valuable insights. Dr. Saustin Mfune, the possibilities and encouragement to start writing came from you. Thank you. Dr. Zebron Ncube, I am a product of both your classroom and your pew, thank you for the many years of learning from you. Joshua Maponga and Donny Marandure, thanks for your wise uncensored encouragements and for keeping constant the joy of working for the Lord. Edmore Mangena, the laughter and your friendship came in handy. Robert Tuvako and Loyce Okelo your friendship and encouragements were priceless. Isaac Kubvoruno, as we sang together since we were boys, uneraseable memories were were being created. Thank you. Abel Sitali you are a friend indeed, thank you for always being there. Gift Mweemba, your friendship and wisdom are a gift to me from God. Pastor Ian Hartley, and Lena Nozizwe, thanks for reading the manuscript and offering wise counsel and encouragement. Dr. Baraka Muganda, it was a privilege to have been one of your youths as I was growing up, and to have you write the foreword in my book is an honor. Thank you. To the district of Chiwundura, Central Zimbabwe, and my colleagues at the great Central Zimbabwe Conference, my tour of duty officially started there, and all that I call experience is because of my interaction with the wonderful people there. Thank you for teaching me the work of ministry. To Ian Phiri and the staff at Teach Services, thank you for giving wings to my thoughts. The list of those that helped enrich my Christian walk over the years is unending. Thank you all.

Simba

FOREWORD

It takes one's creativity and photographic mind to draw spiritual lessons from such a popular film like "Lion King."

Simbarashe Charumbira, has done an outstanding work in making this film so vivid and alive by drawing gospel lessons from it. He has broken down the story of Simba, and somehow coincided it with not only the gospel of Jesus but with how the devil came about, and his intentions with regards to our souls. The book takes the reader from Genesis through to Revelation in a very practical way.

The Gospel in the Lion King addresses the problem of sin and how one can be easily seduced by it in the same way Mufasa's brother Scar goes about with his deceptive intentions to gain the kingdom. Each chapter increases the reader's anticipation of how the book will end and at the same time enjoy the memorable scenes from the film, "Lion King." With the "Lion King" story being the parable, Simbarashe has managed to make parallelism between the film and the gospel concepts as found in the Bible and he makes incredible sense. This book takes you from Genesis to Revelation – from humankind's fall to our restoration.

The author has also done an incredible job of exegeting scripture from the Bible, connecting it with real life events and the life of "Simba." This book is worth reading! Since the parallelism stems from the film "Lion King," in this case, it will make more sense if the reader watches the film first and then explore the rich gospel concepts that have been included in the book. You will definitely enjoy the occasional flashbacks of the scenes from "Lion King's" "Simba."

Read it! Make it part of your spiritual journey.

Baraka G. Muganda
World Youth Director
Silver Spring, Maryland, United States
March, 2008

INTRODUCTION

"Have you watched the Lion King?" I kept being asked. "Not yet," I would answer. But one day I decided to rent the movie and watch this character called by my name. Fascinating it was, hilarious were the characters, especially when I think of Timon's laughter, but one thing caught my attention more – the fact that right away, I noticed the movie replicated the story of the gospel. Right then and there, I thought, "I must write a book on the gospel in the Lion King."

It would turn out to be years before I actually put my thoughts on paper, but I remembered the story of the children of Israel, as they crossed the Jordan with Joshua, that God blesses what you do. The command was clear, the Priests carrying the Ark of the Covenant must dip the soles of their feet into the water and then it will be parted, but not before. (Joshua 3:13) As long as the twelve men had not by faith put their feet forward into the river, the waters would not part. Only after they did, would the waters of the Jordan part and make it possible for the Israelites to pass. God blesses what you do and not what you think you must do. The result is the book you are now holding. This book is not written in order to promote the movie "The Lion King," but it is simply written in order to share the story of the gospel in response to a movie that millions have watched.

The "Lion King" is the story of a young cub, "Simba," born to one King Mufasa of Pride Lands. Upon the birth of Simba, Scar, the King's brother automatically goes to second place in line to the throne. Thus Scar plots to kill Simba and his father and he succeeds to kill the King. Prince Simba runs away from Pride Lands in shame after being made to believe by his uncle Scar that the father's death was his fault, and Scar becomes King. While in exile, Simba meets Pumba and Timon who become his close buddies until he's grown up. Simba is then persuaded to return home and battle with uncle

Scar, win the kingdom back, and take his proper place in the circle of life.

You will notice that in my interpretation of the story, the character of Simba is a type of both Jesus and humankind depending on the scene. Hopefully, through this famous story someone will be ushered into the kingdom of God before probation closes.

CHAPTER 1

UNTO US A SON IS BORN

When an anticipated child is born, it is always a source of joy to the parents and friends. There is even much more joy if the child may be the first one. In the case of most African families, if the first child is a boy, there is even more jubilation. One cannot only imagine, but see the joy in King Mufasa, King of the animal kingdom in Pride Lands, an African Savanna. Much like the biblical renditions, "unto us a child is born," a son is born into the house of the king. All the animal kingdom marches with jubilation as they come to the king's palace to celebrate the birth of Simba.

The giraffe, the zebra, the ant, the elephant, the leopard, the stork, the rabbit, the deer, the whole animal kingdom, and the birds of the skies come to the king's palace in their dozens, marching as they sing the sweet and melodious tune, the "Circle of Life." It is exhilarating to see the order of the service as Zazu arrives and is greeted by the king's smile. It marks the highlight of the day when Rafiki marches to the stage; he is the one to anoint baby Simba. From the highest point of the palace, Rafiki lifts the young Simba up after anointing him and the animals impressively bow down in a must-see sight in reverence to the newborn king.

Being the king's first born; Simba is heir apparent to the throne. The marching of the animal kingdom from far and wide appears to replicate the Savior's birth. Two thousand years ago, the angels sang a song as the King was born in Bethlehem, "Glory to God in the highest, and on earth peace, good will toward men" (Luke 2:14). Many in the world had been studying and anticipating the coming of the Messiah, and "in the fullness of time, Christ was born." The Old Testament is pregnant with the promises of Jesus the Messiah, and in the New Testament, He is not only born but becomes the fulfillment of the promise. In fact the Bible, though written over a span of fifteen hundred years by different authors, is one love story. It centers upon this one Man who loved the human race so much that He would even risk His throne in heaven to come down to earth and become a Man. In the Old Testament, humanity sinned, and there was need of a Savior. Humans could not save themselves; we needed a Savior. The good news is that as soon as there was sin, there was a Savior. Jesus the Messiah had put a plan in place that should man sin, He would come down and die for us. Meanwhile, while they awaited the promise of a Savior, they were to make lamb sacrifices for the forgiveness of their sins in place of the real Lamb that would come. The salvation of the people in the Old Testament was *subject* to the coming of the Messiah to die on the cross. In the New Testament and beyond, we are all saved *because* of the cross. However, it is important to note that both in the Old and New Testaments, humanity gains unmerited favor. Thus we are all saved by grace, whether it is in the Old or New. If one believes only in the New Testament, it is like someone who bears a child without pregnancy and if one only believes in the Old Testament it is like a woman who gets pregnant but never gives birth.

While the prophecies of the Old Testament pointed to the exact time and manner of the birth of the Messiah, the Jewish leaders did not recognize Him when He came. They had a wrong concept of how and for what reason He would come. Thus, when He came they were not ready and they missed the blessings. In His ministry, Jesus had to remind the people, "My kingdom is not of this world," (John 18:36) but their hearts were not ready. John the Baptist had preached and forewarned the people in preparation of the Messiah, but the Jewish leaders of the time did not seem to get it. They thought that the Messiah would come to liberate them from the Roman rule. However, the wise men from the East while waiting for the king, were visited by angels, told the good tidings and were led to the exact place where he was and made tribute to Him by visiting the manger.

In Pride Lands, when we look at the first scene with hindsight, we see that the day when Simba was born becomes a great day for the whole kingdom because he would later be their savior. It's hard to imagine what would have happened to Pride Lands if Simba had not been born. Simba is born for the salvation of Pride Lands.

As the African saying goes that "the son of a snake is a snake," the son of a king is a king. It only gives joy to know that the human family has been invited to join the ranks of royalty. The mantle had been given to Israel, and when they spurned it, it was extended to the Gentile world and everyone else. The extension has been given in no uncertain terms, "But as many as received Him, to them gave He power to become sons of God . . ."(John 1:12). The invitation couldn't be clearer. All rights and privileges given to the children of the Almighty become instantly ours should we choose to receive His invitation. Moreover, the invitation is worldwide and all inclusive, "For God so loved the world that He gave His only begotten Son, that whosoever believeth in Him should not perish, but have everlasting life." (John 3:16).

No one gets to choose the family into which they will be born, or from which tribe or nationality; even those born into the royal families like my namesake Simba. One has to stick to wherever or whichever family they are born whether rich or poor. Some may have a noble birth (Luke 19:12; 1 Cor 1:26), but others may not have the same privilege. Sometimes one may be born in compromising situations such as having been an unwanted pregnancy and thus left in the open to die, or being born into a poor or intemperate family. Many of these situations predispose a person to a life that is far from the ideal that God requires. It is important to note that God does not hold us accountable for being born sinners or from being predisposed to a sinful life early on in life. However, He holds us accountable for refusing the remedy, Jesus Christ the Savior. He has come to solve the spiritual problems of the human race and His invitation still stands today.

When a baby is born, humans rejoice (John 16:21). However, when a person is *born again*, heaven rejoices, as this is a birth without which one cannot enter into the kingdom of God (John 3:3). At this birth, about which Jesus talked in privacy to Nicodemus, one is then made heir to the throne of God. At the moment of baptism in water and the Spirit, we are ushered in as official recipients of the promise. That is the beginning of the Christian walk, the starting point of the sanctification process. One then is a baby in Christ, and must now be fed with spiritual food and learn to walk by themselves like babies do (1 Corinthians 3:2). As they grow, babies start running on their own. The Christian must be able to grow and walk on their own and even run with the Word. Heaven always rejoices at the birth of new babies in Christ Jesus, and the invitation is extended to you to join the family of God in baptism.

CHAPTER 2

JEALOUS SCAR

Being the king's brother, Scar is next in line to the throne, unless the king bears a son. Thus the ceremony to introduce the heir to the kingdom does not amuse him. One can imagine how jealous the king's brother must be. The fact is that everyone in Pride Lands are in attendance at Simba's anointing; except the king's brother.

Like his name implies, in this world nothing is perfect, there's always a scar somewhere. In Pride Lands, there is Scar, the king's brother, and even in the perfect Garden of Eden, the devil was present. I have also come to realize that in this world, no matter where one goes, there are people that will like you and yet there is almost always going to be someone who does not. They can become a "scar" in your life. Paradoxically, our success in the Christian walk is not dependent on the people that love us, but on those few that do not. The few will either make or break our faith. As Solomon says, "Catch the foxes for us, the little foxes that are ruining the vineyards, While our vineyards are in blossom." (Song of Solomon 2:15) NASB A wise man once said, "A chain is only as strong as its weakest link." Our Christian faith is only as strong as our ability to meet the formidable forces of hatred, jealous, resentment, and the like with success. The greatest temptation we face in this world is self. And the people that do not like us, the "scars" of our lives, have a way of really stretching the limits of our "selves," and the devil has succeeded more times than not. A "scar" is like our own modern Garden of Eden that we must conquer. The good news is that we are not in this by ourselves; Jesus has promised never to leave us. (Hebrews 13:5) In fact, He has already passed the test on our behalf; all we need is to abide in Him and Him in us so that we can say like Paul of old, "it is no longer I who live, but Christ lives in me" (Galatians 2:20). NASB In other words, if I accept Jesus Christ as my personal Savior, then He lives in me and His laws are written on my heart so that the life I now live is in Christ and Him in me. What I do, I do for Him, and since He lives in me, I can face any danger or temptation without fear because Christ faced that already on Calvary. On one hand, Jesus wants us to be like Him, but the devil also is working frantically to make us stay like him since by nature we are sinners like him (Romans 3:23). And he has, in more cases than not, succeeded.

He has been successful in making the human family come to equate power with happiness. In other words, we think that as long as one is not in a position of power, we will not be happy. Thus there is everywhere the pursuit of power "in order to control everyone else." The result of this pursuit for power has been devastating to the human family. Marriages have been broken as a result of the craving for power to control spouses, and wars have been fought between nations because of the pursuit for power. Thousands and millions of lives have needlessly been lost in the pursuit of power. As we look at the results, it is inevitable that we can conclude where this push for the pursuit for power comes from. The devil himself was thrown away from heaven as a result of his pursuit for power. He wanted to overthrow the government of God in heaven and he deceived a third of the angels. In Isaiah the devil says, "I will be like the Most High." (Isaiah 14:14) A creature wanting to be like his Creator? This kind of dealing is not from God. It can only be attributed to the devil and his angels.

Scar mars the story of the lion king as the devil mars the story of the human race. One incident that comes to mind is the meeting that happened between God and His subjects in heaven. Some people bless others by their presence but some "spoil the soup" as soon as they appear. The devil does the latter in the book of Job. The story is about God's people coming to the presence of the Lord, and all is fine until the devil is introduced. "Now there was a day when the sons of God came to present themselves before the LORD, and Satan came also among them." (Job 1:6) From the time Satan is mentioned, we never get to hear about what else transpired in the meeting between God and His subjects. The rest of the 41 chapters dramatically shift back to earth to talk about the bleak results of the devil's jealousy. I have one more reason to go to heaven now, and it is that I would like to hear the rest of the story of what transpired during the rest of that meeting, besides the presence of Satan. On the other hand, as soon as the devil appears in the book of Genesis, the story changes from the bliss of Eden to the bleak toiling of God's people throughout the world's history until the earth shall be made new.

The story of Scar is not encouraging. It brings adrenaline to the onlooker in anticipation of what is going to happen again, but the good news is that there shall come a time when bad news will not be news anymore, for there will be none. When Jesus came and died on the cross, He forever dealt effectively with the problem of sin and thus He invited us His subjects to accept His free grace. Soon and very soon, the scar that has marred this world for generations will be blotted out forevermore.

CHAPTER 3

THE BORDERS OF OUR KINGDOM

Simba is an exciting character to watch. He is energetic; he arises in the morning to wake his dad up so they can go for a prearranged touring session. On the tour, King Mufasa gives Simba the valuable lessons of life, as every father must do, and also royal information since he will be the next king. He shows Simba the extent to which their kingdom goes and the borders within their jurisdiction. One very important lesson for one to learn early on in life is to know that there are boundaries in life, and that if they are crossed, there are inevitable consequences. The sooner one realizes that, the better. Adam and Eve were given boundaries by God and because they crossed them, the world turned out to be what it is today. There are always consequences to one's choices. The speed limits placed on our roads are meant to keep us going and not to slow us down. If the rules of the road are ignored, serious consequences may follow. A woman was found at a serious road accident that had killed her husband and children because her husband would not listen to her as he drove, and failing to even cry, she kept saying, "I told him to let me drive if he was tired but he wouldn't listen."

King Mufasa has to give the lesson of boundaries to his son early on so he can grow up in obedience to them, "That's beyond our borders, you must never go there Simba." Yet another lesson to boundaries is given to the boy. At the suggestion that "I thought a king could do whatever he wants," the answer is precise, "There's more to being king than getting your way all the time." This is an important answer, especially for anyone who later in life gets to positions of influence. Some become governors or CEOs, others presidents, and still others high positions of various kinds. It is important to learn the lesson that the high position is always sweeter when one is leading a happy people. Misuse of power has other consequences, such as stress and restlessness. In the book of Job, God asks the complaining Job to tell Him who made the boundaries of the seas, when he said, "Hitherto shalt thou come, but no further: and here shall thy proud waves be stayed? (Job 38:11)"

God in His wisdom has placed boundaries for all of His creation. The sun rises every morning, the moon shines when it is due, the fruits bud out in their season. However, because of sin, human beings have fallen short of the glory of God. Thus, we continually trample over the boundaries that God has given us. When Adam and Eve sinned, the consequence was that they were moved out of the Garden of Eden; it was now out of bounds to them. A law was given to the human race for them to follow. Abel obeyed the law better than his brother Cain. Instead of using a lamb as an offering to God, Cain used plant produce and God did not accept his offering. He accepted Abel's offering, however, for he had used a lamb as God had informed them. Cain became jealous of his brother and killed him. Thus, Adam and Eve saw the result of their sin first hand. No man had died before that.

As the generations lived on, they became perverse in the eyes of God and He reduced the number of years that a man would live from hundreds to one hundred and twenty. (Gen 6:3)

In order to bring some normalcy to the earth that was so perverted, God instructed Noah, a righteous man to build an ark because He would send rain and they would find shelter. Noah preached for a hundred and twenty years but people mocked and laughed at him. They thought he had gone out of his mind. God always has boundaries of time generously drawn. One Bible writer says, The Lord is not slack concerning His promise, as some count slackness, but is longsuffering toward us, not willing that any should perish but that all should come to repentance" (2 Peter 3:9). NASB

However, many times we disappoint God. We refuse to take Him at His word and when the day of reckoning comes, we are found wanting, but by then it is too late. Whenever God's people got into trouble, it was because they crossed or disobeyed the boundaries set by God.

When the children of Israel came out of Egyptian slavery, they had been there more than four hundred years and they had lost the fervor and the knowledge of God that their ancestors had. Thus God called Moses to Mount Sinai and gave him a table of stone containing ten of the most profound boundaries that God wanted His children to obey. The first four laws deal with how man is to relate to God and the last six have to do with man-to-man relationships.

In the first two laws, God shows that only *He* must be worshipped and honored by His children and none other while the third commandment tells us not to play with the name of the Lord in vain. The fourth commandment had to do with time. It is also a memorial of creation. God says, "Remember the Sabbath day to keep it holy. Six days shalt thou labor and do all your work, but the seventh day is the Lord's...."

God has given us six days to do all our work and out of that, He has asked for only one. Thus, He made it holy. Much like King Mufasa when he says, "You must never go there Simba," the King of the universe says, "You must never work on Sabbath," for it is a holy day unto the Lord. Of all the commandments of God, it is this one that has especially not been followed well. In fact, it has been changed. Many have taken the first day of the week as their Sabbath instead of the seventh, arguing that Jesus rose from the dead on Sunday. This came about chiefly because the church in the Dark Ages changed the day of worship from Sabbath to Sunday. Many today have been deceived that Sunday is the true day of worship but the Bible and what God constituted at the beginning does not change.

The boundaries that God has placed for the human race are there for a reason, and many of the world's population live in misery simply because we have not heeded to the call of obedience to our Creator. The good news is that God's arms are still wide open right now calling His children to come under His wings. Accepting Jesus as your Lord and Savior is the best way to have

Him help you keep His boundaries like the apostle Paul teaches, "It is no longer I that lives but Christ lives in me" (Galatians 2:20).

CHAPTER 4

PLAYING IN THE DANGER ZONE

Knowing that his brother was unhappy with the arrival of Simba, it would be correct to assume that King Mufasa would not want Simba near Scar at any time. However, as the history unfolds, little, unsuspecting Simba gets to meet with Uncle Scar and it turns out that Uncle Scar has an agenda much like the old serpent of Genesis 3, to have Simba break the law and die. Power is the underlying current in the transactions that transpire.

Uncle Scar's agenda is certain; to ascend the throne once Simba is eliminated. He has always been in line to the throne as long as Simba was not born, but those dreams have now been shattered at the arrival of the king's son. Thus in order to ascend the throne, Simba must be smartly eliminated by his own doing, yet without him suspecting anything. The devil has been thrown to earth as a result of wanting to take the place of God in heaven, and because Adam is God's son, he must be deceived, in order that should he fail, all earth may be under Satan's control forever. However, much like Simba, unsuspecting Eve plays into the hands of the archenemy and she is deceived. Uncle Scar uses the method that works with most kids—creating curiosity, and now Simba cannot wait to go and see the lion's graveyard, which is beyond the point of where he must not cross.

The devil has ever used curiosity to lure most of God's children into sin. He exaggerates the extent to which satisfaction would be found should they engage in the kind of sin he's luring them to. Before engaging in the act, the loss of not committing the sin looks so great as opposed to the satisfaction of doing it. Thus, many are lured into sin and yet to their surprise, often they discover that sin is not so great after all. However, they may already be in big trouble and the results of it are inevitable.

The other day I was walking in the nearest town to the district that I was pastoring and I met one young woman that used to be in the same youth group with me. She told me she was married now and how she had moved to that town. When I asked her if her husband was a Christian, she echoed what most Christian girls think. "The guys in the church are just the same as the ones in the world. So it's just the same." "Well," I said, "but remember we were taught to marry believers and all." She said she was content, and he allowed her to go to church so he was fine. Incidentally, a few months later I met the same woman again in the same town and she sadly related to me how her husband was not treating her well and how he no longer wanted her to attend church.

Most Christians know the parameters and how they should conduct themselves, but for some reason, the devil lures them with many enticements. In my short life, I have seen innocent girls lured by handsome and nice-talking men into premarital sex. As they talk about it, thinking they are in love, they tend to anticipate great things. However, the inevitable has often happened. They get pregnant at an early age. They may have no job, their parents are humiliated, and their guilt is unsurpassable. When they look at friends and family, their faces seem to reflect, "we told you so." The luring man has no job and he has run away. Lately, the girls may not get pregnant but the guilty feelings follow them all the way. Then, they realize the magnitude of the folly of their decision. They played in the danger zone.

Simba takes Nala with him and together they break the king's explicit commandment, "You should never go there Simba." And, as it should be, the consequences of disobedience are inevitable. Much like Adam and Eve, they find themselves in the hands of hungry hyenas and thus they need a Savior. Once we place ourselves in the hands of the enemy, we place ourselves in great danger of disobedience and thus the Bible warns us to "avoid the appearance of evil." (1 Thessalonians 5:22) Zazu is always there for Simba and thus it is with the Holy Spirit and angels. They are always a present help in time of need. When we place ourselves in danger, God does not abandon us, He sends the angels to protect us and the Holy Spirit is always appealing to our senses to not do foolish things.

Almost immediately after they disobey, Simba and Nala find themselves in danger. The hungry, salivating hyenas are ready to have them for dinner. Yet the reason they are there in the first place is because of Simba's conversation with Scar. Scar paints a picture for Simba that only the brave go to the elephant graveyard. He implies that if one does not go to the yard they are not brave, but Simba, the king's son, is brave like his father, and all brave lions do daring things, so he must venture and go and show his bravado despite an explicit order from his father not to go there. The Serpent in Eden made sure to eat the fruit while Eve looked at him as proof that only the brave, and those that would know good and evil, just like God, would eat the fruit. God was only barring them from the fruit because He did not want them to be like Him. Yet the Serpent ate of the fruit and did not die. Thus, Eve too would not die as God said.

As the serpent spoke to Eve, he made sure to appeal to all the senses to lure the lady of Eden. By talking to Eve, he used the sense of hearing, by touching the fruit without any apparent repercussions, he appealed to Eve's sense of touch. While talking with Eve, the serpent helped Eve see the fruit at a closer range than ever before and it looked normal, just like any other fruit of the garden. By the time the serpent used the sense of taste, one would be sure the rest of the senses had already been activated in Eve's mind; she was ready to follow the whims of the devil. Thus the serpent had to illustrate to Eve how it was possible to taste the fruit and not die, (Genesis 3:4) and as soon as she tasted that fruit, sin entered into the world, thus contaminating it and calling for the Son of God, Jesus, to come and repair the damage.

Today, the devil has not changed. He still is succeeding in deceiving the human family using our five senses. One of the most effective methods of deception the devil has used over the centuries has been the sense of sight, as the saying goes, "seeing is believing," our sense of sight has been exploited and will cause many to lose eternal life. Many have looked on as false prophets perform miracles and believed them despite the warning from God to "test every spirit." (1 John 4:1). The sense of sight has been exploited especially by the introduction of the television. This has been an abused avenue to the soul for sure. In order to "smartly" appeal to people's dollars, the advertising community uses nearly naked women or sexual innuendo on the television screen, and this could be hardly in line with God's will. Many have looked on as the wicked prosper and the righteous suffer and thus lost their trust in God. Yet Jesus made it clear that His kingdom is not of this world (John 18:36). Thus, if we are His children, we would not be worried about the prosperity of this world. We should learn from one who had it all: power, riches, women, wisdom, and everything and anything he wanted. He writes in unequivocal terms, "vanity of vanities; all is vanity" (Ecclesiastes 1:2, 14).

Another sense that God graciously gave us for use is the sense of hearing. It is hard to imagine how the world would be without the sense of hearing. Not all the harmonious music we hear would be a part of our lives. Communication would be more difficult. Yet, good as it is, the devil has also put unfiltered waves of wickedness into it. Much as "faith comes by hearing," so is wickedness. The music that most people listen to is far from nobility; it even denigrates the works of God and praises the devil. Yet we find it so easy and are eager to listen to all that. Most people have no idea that the secular music we listen to is designed in such a way that it suppresses the frontal lobe of the brain, the citadel of our decision making. Thus many unwise decisions have been made at the intoxication of secular music. On the other hand, cheap talk and boasting are leading us far from God's ideal for our lives. The five senses are interdependent and always work well together. Once one is exploited, it usually affects the others. When the eyes have been deceived, then we want to hear, then touch, smell, and speak.

On the other hand, a noble use of one of the senses can lead a person in the right direction. When we listen to the word of God, then it will influence us to talk in

Godly language, smell the right things and even touch what is noble. We still have a choice even today. Everyday of our lives, we are put in the same situation as that of Eve. We are to choose between good and evil and God's help is ever present on our side that we should not sin. Only if we listen to the still small voice of the Holy Spirit will we be able to discern right from wrong and follow the Master. This can be achieved with God's help in "guarding the avenues to the soul." The sinfulness of sin is not usually discernible at the spur of the moment when it is committed. However, God is not silent as to the consequences of it as illustrated in the destruction of Sodom and Gomorrah. Soon, fire will destroy the world, but God does not want us to be destroyed in the end, thus even though "all have sinned and come short of the glory of God," (Romans 3:23) and "the wages of sin is death", the gift of God is eternal life through Jesus Christ our Lord (Romans 6:23).

CHAPTER 5

THE PLOT

Scar has been hiding, and intently watching the scene between the hyenas, Simba, and Nala. Thinking that his plot would work, he eagerly waits for the hyenas to devour the king's son only to be disappointed as king Mufasa shows up right on time to rescue his son. Disappointed, Scar's plot number one has failed. Thus, another plan must be imminently executed.

One of the world's evils that has worked to advance the devil's plans has been the use of bribery. Scar shows his true nature as he generously offers a zebra's "drumstick" chunk of meat to the hyenas. This generosity, in a corrupt world, prompts the question right away from the hyenas, "what do you want us to do, kill Mufasa?" This shows how degenerated this world has become. Showing how it is almost becoming impossible for anyone to do anything for another for free. If they did, the recipient quickly thinks, "they must be wanting something." In other words, the hyenas must be wondering, "Why would Scar be giving us this chunk of meat?" And they felt obligated to give something in return. The question also implies that the hyenas know that Scar is Mufasa's nemesis. Why would anyone ask if you wanted to kill your own brother?

Selfishness, greed, and corruption has created over the years a situation where no one can do anything free, even if it may be their rightful duty to do so. The sense of community and togetherness that used to prevail is fast eroding even between brothers. Thus, it is commonplace for a boss to ask for sexual favors at the offer of a job. In far too many countries, it is well known that civil servants will ask for something in return in order to speed up a service as a favor to someone, while doing what would have been their rightful duty in the first place. Travelers will be well aware that ports of entry are a first sign of the magnitude of corruption in a given country. On the one hand, overcharging excise duty for goods brought in is not unheard of and in addition, police bribes are rampant even in the most developed countries. Scar is a good example of how a leader's behavior and conduct is directly linked to the behavior and prosperity of a people. If the leader's integrity is in question, the entity they lead would not prosper. It may take a long time to realize but the results are testimony. To the question about murdering the king, the answer comes swiftly from Scar, "precisely." Thus in the secret chambers of the caves just outside Pride Lands, the plan to kill the king is hatched.

One would have hoped someone would let Scar know that no matter how secret anything they planned would be, it would one day become known. You may hide from your family members, your friends, or bosses or anyone, but you cannot hide from the eye of God for He is able to see even that which is in the heart. Therefore, it is only a matter of time, and however secret, your sins will find you out.

Because of Scar's bribe, he is able to obtain the cooperation of the hyenas. He promises no hunger again when he's king. Just like Lucifer, he has a good voice, singing "Be Prepared," as the hyena kingdom march and give homage to him. All this, Scar manages to do without the knowledge of the king thus the plan seems to work well. When they were plotting to kill Jesus, the Jews worked in secret, "for fear of the people" because they did not have anything valid for which to accuse Jesus. They had to use His statements, which they did not understand, when referring to Himself that if they destroyed "this temple," He would raise it in three days. In this they found reason for imposing on Him the death penalty. All this was done because Jesus was gaining more favor in the eyes of the people than that of the teachers of the law and the Sanhedrin. Thus the plot to kill Jesus, even though difficult to arrange, was finally hatched.

Scar is an example of the evil of greed and power. Scar does not look like a happy person at all. His whole life seems to be bent on how to get to the throne. He's so immersed into the idea that he fails to come for the ceremony of Simba's dedication. In this he shows that as long as he's not king, family is not important. This is the sign of an impaired frontal lobe. Most people do not realize that they may be having symptoms of depression. The kind of life we live will either leave us depressed, or happy and healthy. Scar seems to have been depressed by the birth of Simba; rejection and the wanting to kill a family member is a sign of some form of depression.

The people involved in the plot to kill Jesus were all in some kind of power struggle. The Pharisees were unhappy that He had exposed their hypocrisy and they were not willing to change. The Sadducees were unhappy that by raising Lazarus, He had challenged their assertion that there was no life after death. The Jewish leaders had put too many rigorous unscriptural laws against the law of God and they were not about to lose their influence with the people because a son of a carpenter was a manifestation of the law. They had taught certain things and it would be too humiliating to renounce that which they had always taught as truth. Thus, the only way to avoid trouble was to eliminate Jesus. Judas wanted to precipitate Jesus' rise to power so he could attain a high position through the supposed earthly kingdom of Jesus. It did not come, and when the opportunity of monetary power manifested itself, Judas did what his heart was inclined to do, sell Jesus for some cash. When Judas gave the betrayal kiss to Jesus, his plot was quickly made known by the One who can read the heart. Scar's plot does not get known until a little later, but it comes anyway. Whether someone let's you know about your sin and about your plight sooner or later does not make a difference as long as you do not repent of your sin because the result is the same – eternal loss.

CHAPTER 6

THE KING IS SLAIN

The execution is acted upon as soon as the plot to kill king Mufasa is hatched. Pretending to be a good uncle, Scar takes Simba to the bottomless gorge of one of the dry rivers of Pride Lands promising him a surprise from his father, and a surprise it will be. "Stay here," is the firm command from uncle Scar. "I'll go get your father." Simba obeys and in no time, as soon as the signal is given to the hyenas by uncle Scar, the stampede begins. The hyenas have been instructed to drive the buffalos crazy; a great number of buffalos race away from the hyenas into the gorge where Simba is waiting. The intention is clear, kill Simba in the stampede. Well calculated also, Scar knows King Mufasa will jump in there to rescue Simba and will also be killed. As the stampede begins, Uncle Scar tells King Mufasa, "Simba's down there." And Mufasa, clearly moved by the love of a father, sees no other option but to get down there and rescue his beloved son. There is a great stampede, geared at destroying his son forever, but he himself must go down and save his son; no one else can. Zazu shows him where Simba is hanging onto a tree; the king does not hesitate to leap into the great multitude of the unstoppable buffalos, risking his own life for the life of his son.

One day, Jesus was up in the highest heavens looking down to earth and saw his own children. The human race had been degraded by four thousand years of sin, and in the midst of the stampede of misery, pain, and sorrow, humanity needed a Savior. We could not get out of the situation on our own, and moved by the compassion of a loving Father, Jesus did not hesitate to become "flesh, and dwelt among us, and we beheld His glory, the glory as the only begotten of the Father, full of grace and truth"(John 1:14).

King Mufasa does all He can to save his son and stampeding buffalos make no notice of the king of the

23

jungle. It's a great stampede; they are being effectively driven by the hyenas. Miraculously, the king finds a way to save his son. In the midst of the noise, in one of the most moving scenes of the story, the king shouts to Simba who is hanging onto a branch of a tree, "hold on Simba." Simba is now safe. However, as the king makes a move to escape the dangerous zone and leaps onto one of the rocks, uncle Scar is right there with a chance to save his own brother, but not so. Not this time, the uncle must show his true colors and even though king Mufasa appeals for help, "Scar, brother...," Scar looks at him with an evil eye. The eye of revenge, and as the world watches, thinking that of all the times, even the most degraded of animals would here help their own brother. Little does He know that the object of the stampede was for his death in the first place, and that the culprit is not a stranger, but his very own brother.

Many times as Christians, we often look very far to find the reason for our trouble when the trouble may be in our very own house and often feeding or even sleeping with us. The chance of a lifetime to be king has come, and uncle Scar will not let it go. In a horrible sight to behold, Scar, instead of helping his brother out of the situation, pierces his sharp fangs into the hands of King Mufasa and says these last words to him, "long live the king." A two fold meaning may be attributed to those words. One would be that the people have always said to you "long live the king," but look where you are today. The second would be that "I am now the king and let it be known to you Mufasa that I am king and thus 'long live this king.'" As soon as he says that he throws his own brother into the lake of stampeding animals to die a horrible and undeserving death. Scar's heart of stone is more manifest in this scene than anywhere else. It is placed right there so the world can see the true intention of this power hungry brother.

What a true representation of the scenes of Calvary. That day when Jesus, accompanied by throngs of people, moved on to Golgotha, He was full of compassion. He said to the crying women, "Weep not for me but for yourselves." All that He did was so that the human race may have a place in His kingdom. The songwriter says, "When He was on the cross, I was on His mind."

The stampede of people being pushed by the devil in order to kill Him did not stop Him from going to Golgotha to take the place of the human being. With angry shouts, they cried, "Crucify Him, crucify Him...," and He never said a mumbling word. Having been accused of being an unfair God by Lucifer in heaven, the world must now see the true nature of that accusation. In the beginning when Adam and Eve sinned in the Garden of Eden, they were supposed to die the very instant they ate of the fruit, but even before they were made, the plan of salvation had been put in place in case they sinned. Therefore, as soon as they sinned, the dispensation of grace kicked in. In other words, sin is incompatible with God, but the provision for His son to come and die for fallen humanity made it possible for Adam and Eve to have a second chance. At the same time, if they had been killed at that instance, the devil would have said, "There you go, I told you this God is not fair" But God in His wisdom and love, waited for Calvary in order that the whole universe can see the true nature of sin. At Golgotha, even a skeptic would now see the true nature of the devil's ploy. If he would kill the innocent and sinless Son of God, what will happen to you and me?

Yet it is Calvary that gives us victory. Christ took the place of fallen humanity and He suffered all that we would have suffered. All He asks now from us is to abide in Him by accepting Him as our personal Savior and "He shall direct our paths." When I now do that which is right, and keep His law, I do it not in order to find favor in His sight but because I have found favor in Him and because I love Him. He says, "If you love me, keep my commandments" (John 14:15). NKJV

CHAPTER 7

SCAR IS KING

During the campaign to the hyenas, aspirant King Scar makes a promise that if he becomes king there would be no hunger again. He does that as he generously dishes out the thigh of a zebra and the hyenas go out of their minds. Somehow appetite has a way of removing our thinking caps from our frontal lobes. When food is presented, humanity seems to forget all the promises of God. Scar then manifests a very impressive ceremony of the marching hyenas. To the onlooker, the situation will be just fine in the hands of King Scar. In that impressive ceremony, Scar proves a very good singer, filling the corridors of the caves just outside Pride Lands with his impressive voice with the tune "Be Prepared."

Food has always been used to lure the attention of people and draw them away from God. Scar knows what is on the hyenas' minds; meat, and he delivers. To lure the allegiance of the woman in the Garden of Eden, the devil used food. Said one author, "Just where the ruin began, the work of our redemption must begin. As by the indulgence of appetite Adam fell, so by the denial of appetite Christ must overcome" (Desire of Ages, p.117). Therefore, when Jesus came down to earth and started His ministry, His first temptation was about appetite. In the face of forty days and forty nights without food, He was famished with hunger. The devil took advantage of the situation like he always does. "If you are the son of God, change these stones into bread." But Jesus, with an astute mind, stayed above the devil's plots and overcame the charge. He was the Son of God already, thus He did not need anyone to bring conditions and doubts of whether He was or not.

That day, on our behalf, Christ overcame the sin of appetite which Adam had failed. When the devil says to Jesus just give allegiance to me once and I'll give you all this land that is mine. He was right in a way. Of all the creation that God has made, this world belongs to the devil. He is the prince of this world, the prince of darkness. He has been allowed to play his game here and nowhere else (John 12:31). Appetite had brought King Scar to power on the premise that no one would go hungry in his kingdom. However, the opposite becomes true as reality unfolds. Those who usurp power may enjoy it for a season, but history will prove that the days of their lives are full of trouble. They may have the power they want, but they may not have the peace they need. In King Scar's reign, there is no peace at all as the hyenas have all been placed in charge of positions of power as a reward for their fight to kill king Mufasa. The kingdom is plundered of all its riches as a result.

Hunger and drought are the manifestation and the king does not even notice it despite attempts to alert him of the impending danger of a famine in the land. When we let the devil rule in our lives, the same happens to us in our everyday lives. When presenting a sin, the devil exaggerates the pleasures of getting involved. He does this with an art that has been perfected from six thousand years of experience. However, the end result is sin and misery. The devil has never been our friend and he will never be. In fact he cannot be. But how many of us are deceived by the everyday luring on his side. Even those that seem to have the most allegiance to his deceptions will he cast aside after using them. The movie stars will look bright and attractive until they get so miserable and even end up killing themselves. One actor left this suicide note in 1984 "Let's see if this will do it." *Accidental suicide as he shot himself with a blank-loaded pistol on the set of TV spy show "Cover Up." The concussion forced a chunk of his skull into his brain; he died six days later."*

~~ Jon Erik Hexum, actor, d. October 18, 1984 (www.corsinet.com/braincandy/dying3.html)

As long as the devil is king in our lives we will continue to see more of the same notes such as these:

"I must end it. There's no hope left. I'll be at peace. No one had anything to do with this. My decision totally."

Suicide note.

~~ Freddie Prinze, comedian, d. January 29, 1977 (Ibid)

"Dear World, I am leaving you because I am bored. I feel I have lived long enough. I am leaving you with your worries in this sweet cesspool - good luck."

Suicide note.

~~ George Sanders, British actor, d. April 25, 1972 (Ibid)

This reminds me of the story of Jacob and Laban. Having worked for his wives for seven years and his animals for six, the Bible minces no words, "And Jacob saw the countenance of Laban, and indeed it was not favorable toward him as before."(Genesis 31:2) The devil can look like he's your friend when enticing you to sin, however, no sooner than you sin does he do a good job of abandoning you.

When we look at the world today, there is no doubt who is in charge of the situation. The devil is at work in the world. No wonder there are hurricanes, whirlwinds, floods, hunger, starvation, poverty and the many negatives in the world today. But the good news is found in Luke 21:28 "And when these things begin to come to pass, then look up, and lift up your heads; for your redemption draweth nigh." When we have seen the sinfulness of sin then it is easier to understand the goodness of the good news of Jesus. Soon, the deliverance that we have been waiting for will arrive. Many today are in need of redemption but they are looking for it in all the wrong places, but thank God only through Jesus Christ can we get true redemption. Even the songwriter saw it and said, "It's always darkest before the dawn." When it seems insurmountable, behold redemption comes. The good news is that "For yet a little while, and He that shall come will come and will not tarry." (Hebrews 10:37)

CHAPTER 8

HAKUNA MATATA

Simba runs away to a far land and the hyenas quit pursuing him. He gets tired and passes out on a dry plain. The scavengers of the air are good at clearing anything they consider a mess to the earth and Simba is about to be eaten alive in his sleep. Providentially, however, just as soon as the scavengers spot the young cub and are ready to eat him up, Pumba and Timon arrive to his rescue. Taking a chance at rescuing a lion, they take Simba to their home. He revives, but because he's so depressed at what he had been made to believe had been a great tragedy of his own making, he plans on leaving these two strangers.

The strangers take him by surprise and teach him the phrase, "hakuna matata." This is a phrase in the Kiswahili language of East Africa meaning no worries, or no problem. Being their motto, Pumba and Timon take Simba for a lesson on hakuna matata and he embraces it. This sounds like the story of the prodigal son in Luke 15. In this case, even before the father dies, the son asks for his portion of the inheritance so that he can use it now. The father is troubled at that but he gives it to him anyhow. The son goes to a far country and spends all he had been given gluttonously. Upon being introduced to insects for food, Simba loses his appetite. He has never eaten that kind of food in his life. It is not the food that lions eat, but in a snake and Eve-like manner, Pumba and Timon demonstrate to him that the insects are good for food. Simba tastes it and exclaims, "It's satisfying." He is officially entered and welcomed in the land of "hakuna matata."

He lives there for some years, going from place to place in the same area and enjoying all that the land had to give. The land has scenes of unsurpassed beauty and Simba, Pumba and Timon live a happy, worry free, no rules kind of life. Simba grows up and his hair grows like that of all male lions. The fact that he is a lion can never be hidden from anyone. No matter how much he adjusts to Pumba and Timon's lifestyle, he remains not only a lion, but a son of the lion king. Many of us have grown in the knowledge of Jesus Christ, lived the life of a Christian, and learned that we are "a chosen generation, a royal priesthood, a holy nation, His own special people, that [we] may proclaim the praises of Him who called [us] out of darkness into His marvelous light" (1 Peter 2:9) NKJV

However, we have met some "friends" who not only told us, but even demonstrated to us how to have the good life, a life of perceivably "no problems" and no rules. It looks like fun to get involved in and it almost seems like we have been deprived due to our earlier years of what we may perceive to have been parental control and depravity. Now we must do all we want without anyone controlling what we do. In this instance, it is important to remember that here lies the "father of lies" (John 8:44), the devil, who is good at exaggerating the perceived good and blackening our good past. Just like the prodigal son, many get involved in the wooing of this world and start a life that is not pleasing to God. God's laws have been restricting their movement and now they are free to do all they want. At this time, when so called freedom has been attained, the person gets involved in many unbecoming issues such as drugs, pride, and slander, disobedience to parents, sexual immorality, and loving pleasure more than they love God.

The prodigal son may have left for a far away country, but many of us will not have to leave to a far away country, but do the things that place us very far away from God. Isaiah 59:2 says, "But your iniquities have separated you from your God; your sins have hidden his face from you, so that he will not hear." NKJV Today's Christians embrace a lostness that combines the likes of both the prodigal son and his elder brother who did not go to a far country but instead was lost while at home. This is manifest in the fact that when his prodigal brother comes back and the father slaughters a cow for him, the elder brother is unhappy. His argument, though befitting the mind of the world and proper justice, is far away from the mind of a follower of Jesus Christ. He must be taught that mercy overrides justice.

Many of the so called believers may in fact be lost while in the church. If a person loses their way in their Christian walk, it is hard for some to accept them when they come back to the church. They are labeled and would be lucky to get off the scarred label for the rest of their lives. This may not be said, but it can sure be manifested from the fact that, said 'come back Christians' may sometimes have barred themselves away from certain privileges such as being elected to certain positions in the church like an elder or deacon or deaconess. This is because the elder brother-like members' attitude toward the prodigal is hard to change when they have to nominate them to a position in the church.

Being lost in the church comes in various forms. The other day a friend and I visited a church in my area and having made a presentation to a group of women in the church that meet during the week, I asked one of the women in charge to offer prayer, and she was not hesitant to let us know "I'm not good at that." Not only could she not pray as she told us later, but she commented, "We do not usually pray here." The idea behind their not praying was, as she explained, that some women come from the community to the church and they do not necessarily want to pray and so they do not want to offend them lest they will not return to find the help they need. One would think that it should have been the opposite. Of all places, the church is where anyone should find comfort in prayer. All that come to church know that church people pray to God and when church people deprive them of that privilege, they are not only doing a disfavor to that person, but more so to God. Only if people could be taught to have a relationship with God could they understand the deep things that He has in store for us and we would live a much happier life than the "hakuna matata" kind of life.

If we do not surrender our lives to God, the devil will fill the void that only God is supposed to fill. Therefore the love of pleasure has in fact brought worldliness right into the church. Many of the things that never used to be done in any Christian church are today not only prevalent but openly practiced in the church. No wonder John warned, "Love not the world, neither the things that are in the world. If any man love the world, the love of the Father is not in him."(1 John 2:15) Worldly music, as an example, has come right to the doorsteps of the church and has been embraced in the form of "Christian rock," "Christian jazz," or any other kind of worldly music. When I was growing up, it was very easy to distinguish secular music from sacred. Now they both sound the same, all a person has to do is listen to the words if they can be heard. If there is the name Jesus, or if there is some reference to a biblical name or event or Christian jargon, then it is said to be Christian music.

One would argue that what makes music is not only the lyrics, but the accompanying sound of it. If it were only the lyrics that mattered, then one would simply repeat them. In this form therefore, the devil has found a way of enslaving us while in the very place that should liberate us from him – the church. The devil lie to us however, is that a person who lives a life outside of God will be happy. Many people have heeded the call to find a life with "no problems," and found themselves having to contend with problems; divorce that is tearing families away, envy, anger, jealousy, lack of respect, wayward children, and unpeaceful lives in general. In short, there is no life such as "hakuna matata." It has been said that as long as we are this side of heaven, death and taxes are sure. A life of "hakuna matata" will only be witnessed by those that will be faithful till the end. Only when we get to the pearly gates will we be able to say "hakuna matata" in the real sense of the phrase except it shall be translated into the heavenly language.

CHAPTER 9

THE GODS IN HEAVEN

In one of the funniest scenes in the Lion King, Simba, Pumba, and Timon have had their supper and are lying down relaxing on the grass enjoying the cool breeze of the night. They are all looking upward to the skies. Simba's burp opens the scene and it's commended by Pumba, to which Simba thanks him. As one begins to enjoy the company of the trio as they look up to heaven, Pumba is inspired to ask Timon a question about the stars in heaven. He asks, "Have you ever wondered what those are?" Their conversation goes philosophical and they ask Simba's opinion. Not wanting to look foolish, he shies away but they press him. At this time, "inspiration," so to say, comes to Simba as he remembers his father's teaching. Says Simba, "Someone once told me the kings of the past are up there watching over us." This brings one of the funniest responses as Timon is prompted to bring out his unique laughter. "You mean a bunch of dead guys are up there watching over us?"

As one watches the conversation, it is easy to laugh off and enjoy the trio's discourse. However, there is a lot of implications in the scene. Timon and Pumba's reaction is representative of millions of people who have no idea that there is a God in heaven watching over us. Many people have lost sight of who they are because they do not know where they come from. Simba's answer may be biblically flawed because of what he had been taught.

African traditional religion, like many other world religions teaches that the spirits of our fathers are watching over us. This implies that even though our ancestors are dead, they are not really dead; only their flesh is dead, their spirits are watching over us. In traditional African religion, the gods can be called by having a ceremony that includes the hard beating of drums and singing and dancing. Then the spirit medium suddenly gets possessed and gets into a trance and starts speaking to the people as if it's the dead father giving warnings to the family and sometimes expressing dissatisfaction with certain things and so on. These manifestations happen in real life and thus many have been led to believe that their ancestors are alive and well in their spirits.

The Bible is not silent about spirits and mediums. Saul, the first king of Israel, having mounted the army of Israel near Mount Gilboa, had wanted to hear a word from the Lord on whether Israel would make it in the impeding battle. However, because he had apostatized, the Lord would not answer him and Samuel the prophet who used to counsel him was now dead. Saul, with a heavy heart, wished Samuel were alive, thus he contacted a spirit medium. "Bring up Samuel for me," the king requested and a spirit came and spoke with Saul. The spirit told King Saul that Israel would lose and that he and his sons would die in the battle (1 Samuel 28). Because the predictions came true, one wonders if the spirit was really the true Samuel since God condemned the medium.

Scripture is clear on this subject, that only God is immortal, (1 Timothy 1: 17, 1 Timothy 6:16) and humans are mortal. Job says, man "comes forth like a flower and fades away; he flees like a shadow and does not continue." (Job 14:2) NKJV David says humans are "but flesh, a breath that passes away and does not come again" (Psalm. 78:39). NKJV In fact, after sin, God removed man from the garden of Eden "lest he put out his hand and take also of the tree of life and live forever"(Gen 3:22). NKJV When a person dies, says the Bible, he is asleep. In other words a person is in an unconscious state awaiting the resurrection of the dead at the last trumpet (Luke 15:51-55). The kings of Israel are described as asleep in the Old Testament (1 Kings 2:10; 11:43; 14:20,31; 15:8 etc.).

The New Testament reveals the same, such as when Jesus raised Jairus' daughter (Matt 9:24; Mark 5:39) and when Jesus raised Lazarus from the dead (John 11:11-14). Ecclesiastes puts it even more clearly "for the living know that they will die; but the dead know nothing, and they have no more reward, for the memory of them is forgotten" (Eccl 9:5). NKJV The notion that the dead are watching over us is one of the greatest lies ever told and it stems from the father of lies on the very first lie told to deceive Eve in the Garden of Eden, "You shall not surely die." It was here that the doctrine of the immortality of the soul was founded. Today, many ministers teach their members that their dead loved ones have gone to heaven. I overheard one minister saying, "That's the beauty of preaching at a funeral, when you tell them that their loved one has gone up to heaven."

It sounds good to hear but the scriptures do not support it. That doctrine is in fact saying that a person does not die, but goes to heaven instead. One would ask, if humans went to heaven at death, why would we be so afraid of death? I am sure it would be a much welcome relief to go quickly to the pearly gates. If it were true, Why would Jesus be coming back the second time? In addition, if death were not such a bad thing, why would it need to be thrown into the lake of fire on the last day? (Revelation 20:14) Heaven would not be so much of a joy for anyone going there to watch their relatives crushed by the pangs of death and weeping and wailing for them. If one would think of it, Jesus would have been very cruel to resurrect Lazarus because, if it were true, He would have literally removed him from heaven to come back to this terrible earth.

One would need to go and tell Simba, Pumba and Timon that there is a God in heaven watching over us and that soon He will come again to take all His loved ones home, and at that time, and only then will the dead rise, some to eternal life and others to eternal damnation. A person's fate is sealed at death because there is no repentance after death.

CHAPTER 10

EQUALLY YOKED

Simba leaves Pride Rock when he is young and he literally grows up with Pumba and Timon. Little does he know that his best friend Nala is being raised just for him. Pumba and Timon are busy singing along the way on their worry free life, and Pumba is distracted by a delicious insect and starts courting its course to get it. Meanwhile, Nala is hunting for food since there is nothing left in Pride Rock at the hands of Scar and the hyenas. All of a sudden, Pumba is in trouble. He and Timon are almost dead meat as soon as Nala catches them but Simba providentially comes to their rescue. It's at this time that Simba realizes it's Nala and there starts the conversation that leads to a romantic getaway in the paradise land of "hakuna matata."

What a fit that becomes. It would have been inconceivable for Simba to get a girl who is not a lion. For him it works out that he not only gets married to a lion, but he gets married to his friend from Pride Rock. When Abraham sought a wife for his son, he sent his servant back to his in-laws. "Please, put your hand under my thigh, and I will make you swear by the Lord the God of heaven and the God of the earth, that you will not take a wife for my son from the daughters of the Canaanites, among whom I dwell; but you shall go to my country and to my family, and take a wife for my son Isaac" (Gen 24:2-4). NKJV Getting a wife that feared the Lord for his son was so important for Abraham because he was a son of the promise.

Earlier on, God had appeared to Abraham and said, "'Look now toward heaven, and count the stars if you are able to number them.' And He said to him, 'so shall your descendants be'" (Gen 15:5). NKJV However, Sarai, Abraham's wife, saw that she was barren and gave Hagai her maidservant to Abram (before his name was changed to Abraham) for a wife, saying, "Perhaps I shall obtain children by her." (Gen 16:2) NKJV and she bore a son and named him Ishmael. However, when God later makes a covenant between him and Abraham he says about Ishmael, "I will make him a great nation. But my covenant I will establish with Isaac, whom Sarah (Sarai's new name) shall bear to you at this set time next year" (Gen 17: 20, 21). NKJV

Isaac was a son of the promise and he must be the progenitor of a generation that God had promised Abraham. Should he get a wife from the Canaanites, chances are high that she would have diverted his attention from the Lord. It has been seen a great many times that when a Godly man takes a wife that does not fear the God of heaven, she will likely divert his attention from the Lord. King Ahab of Israel is one example, (1 Kings 21) also king Solomon, (1 Kings 11:1-4) and Samson and Delilah (Judges). The same principle applies to Godly women marrying ungodly men. God's plan is that when a man marries a woman, they should live together till death do them part. Because of the importance of being of one mind as far as the fear of the Lord is concerned, an apostate spouse would only bring calamity and reproach to the household of the believer.

We are a "chosen generation, a royal priesthood, a holy nation," His own special people, but the life goals of a spouse that does not fear God are different and far away from God's plan for humans. Thus exhorting the Corinthians to be holy, not only in marriage but in all of life's alliances, Paul says, "Do not be unequally yoked together with unbelievers. For what fellowship has righteousness with lawlessness? And what communion has light with darkness? And what accord has Christ with Belial? Or what part has a believer with and unbeliever?" (2 Corinthians 6:14) NKJV

Many a young person would say, "I will convert her/him" but that is not the way God planned conversion. God never asked us to marry and baptize them but to preach and baptize them. They should convert because they love God (Romans 2:4) not because they love you. In today's world, there has been so much divorce that it has ceased to be alarming. However, for the couples that stay together the longest, one of the major contributing factors is that they are of the same religious faith. Beyond the outside beauty, there is a life to be lived. One must live with their spouse everyday of their lives. No matter how beautiful the spouse may be, if they are not of the same mind especially on religious terms, they are going to have big trouble. Chances are they will live a contentious life or their marriage will not last.

God hates divorce (Malachi2:16) and the only reason we can divorce is if one of the spouses gets into adultery. Even then, He says because of the hardening of our hearts. In other words, God wishes that couples stay together for life as long as they are married. Too many times the reason for divorce has been because of so called "irreconcilable differences," and this has led many to get into trial and error marriages, "if it does not work, I'll get out of it." In fact, it is alarming that many Christians are so very ignorant of this portion of God's requirement in marriage.

At one time, a young girl I knew got married to a certain young man. Because there had not been a lot of preparation for the marriage and they did not know each other very well, the relatives were talking about it. Like many concerned relations would, they discussed the plans the couple had made, and one of them said, "She should wait because she does not know how far this marriage will go in the first place." While the intentions of that statement may be good, the rationale behind it is flawed. It is built on the premise that "if there is seeming disagreement, then I'm out."

God created marriage and in His plan for marriage, there are no ifs and no conditions for staying the course. One must stay in it for life, or we have many single parents raising children on their own needlessly. One could not avoid it if they were brought to singleness because of the death of a spouse, but far too many singles are a result of divorce. On the other hand, it is important to note that for innocent spouses, they could not help but accept the situation. Thus, they had to separate and one can only sympathize. If only today's youth would grasp the hand of God and learn God's principles of marriage, how many homes would be saved from this distress?

As an unmarried young man myself, God forbid that I should look only at the beauty of the outside and get a woman for a wife only on that premise. Simba has taught me to go back to my people, the children of Abraham by faith, the believers, and find a Nala there.

CHAPTER 11

WHEN HE CAME TO HIS SENSES

Simba literally grows up in the hands of Pumba and Timon. When he arrives at "Hakuna Matata land, he has not hairs on his neck yet, but at the hands of Pumba and Timon, Simba grows into manhood. While sitting and relaxing one evening after a meal, the trio get into a conversation that marks the turning point of the king's son. As Pumba and Timon talk about the meaning of the stars in the heavens, Simba listens. The question is then turned to him, he answers to the best of his knowledge. "Somebody once told me that the great kings of the past are up there watching over us" When Simba mentions "somebody" he inevitably thought about his father because it was he that had taught him about the meaning of the stars and other lessons of life.

One wonders what Simba is thinking at this point as he talks about his father and even mentions that "the great kings of the past are up there watching over us." It is at that moment that it dawns upon him that should this statement be true, according to the popular theory of the dead watching on us, his own father, one of the great kings of the past, must have been watching over him. Even as Pumba and Timon relax on the grass, Simba stands up to go and look into the sky as if something has just begun to trouble his mind.

This is a story reminiscent of the biblical story of King Nebuchadnezzar. One day as he was walking on top of the magnificent walls of the city of Babylon, "The king reflected and said, 'is this not Babylon the great, which I myself have built as a royal residence by the might of my power and for the glory of my majesty?' While the word was in the king's mouth, a voice came from heaven, saying, 'King Nebuchadnezzar, to you it is declared: sovereignty has been removed from you, and you will be driven away from mankind, and your dwelling place will be with the beasts of the field. You will be given grass to eat like cattle, and seven periods of time will pass over you, until you recognize that the Most High is ruler over the realm of mankind and bestows it on whomever He wishes'" (Daniel 4:30-32). NASB The Bible records that immediately King Nebuchadnezzar became like one of the animals and he fed on grass for the next seven years. "...His body was drenched with the dew of heaven, until his hair had grown like eagles' feathers and his nails like birds' claws" (Daniel 4:33). NASB

Interestingly, at the end of that period, the king himself gives testimony to the effect, "I, Nebuchadnezzar, raised my eyes toward heaven, and my reason returned to me, and I blessed the Most High and praised and honored Him who lives forever; for His dominion is an everlasting dominion, and his kingdom endures from generation to generation." (vs 34) Note the occasion for Nebuchadnezzar's return to normalcy; it was only when he had "raised [his] eyes toward heaven" that he came to his senses. He explains it more clearly himself, "At that time my reason returned to me. And my majesty and splendor were restored to me for the glory of my kingdom, and my counselors and my nobles began seeking me out; so I was reestablished in my sovereignty, and surpassing greatness was added to me. Now I Nebuchadnezzar praise, exalt, and honor the King of heaven, for all His works are true and His ways just, and He is able to humble those who walk with pride" (Daniel 4:36, 37). NASB

Interestingly, it is when Simba lifts up his eyes to the heavens to his perceived gods and sees stars that he comes to his senses. Jesus in Luke 15 tells the story of a young man who thought he would get his inheritance even before the father died and upon receiving his portion of the inheritance, he went to a far country and began spending the dollars with loose living. After he had spent all his possessions, there was a famine in the land, thus he found a job with one of the men of the land feeding swine. He longed to fill his stomach with what the swines ate. Take note, the Bible is straight forward, "But when he came to his senses, he said, "how many of my father's hired men have more than enough bread, but I am dying here with hunger. I will set up and go to my father, and will say to him, Father, I have sinned against heaven, and in your sight; I am no longer worthy to be called your son; make me as one of your hired men. So he got up and came to his father, But while he was still a long way off, his father saw him, and felt compassion for him, and ran and embraced him, and kissed him" (Luke 15:17-20). NASB

These and other stories are recorded in the Bible to help us grasp the extent of God's love for his children. When one runs away from the will of God, there is a conscience that troubles; and ignoring it dulls the senses until the sin no longer seems wrong. Therefore, a person continues in those acts having suppressed the frontal lobe, the citadel of decision-making.

Simba's thoughts trouble him after speaking with Nala, but one important step helps his final decision, he realizes his sinfulness. He thinks he's responsible for his father's death; thus, he looks up to the sky and rants, "It's my fault." The first step to the rehabilitation of a sinner in God's eyes is the realization that "I am a sinner." But in His love, God is never wearied. He continues to talk to us with that still, small voice that urges us to change our wrong course of action. Thus, it is only when one comes to their senses that a person can run back to God and do His biddings. Usually it is at that time that a person breaks down, having realized what they have done to God and to themselves.

When Simon Peter denied the Lord three times, it is when he looked at the Savior and saw His love that he came to his senses and remembered what Jesus had told him, "Before the cock cries, you shall deny me three times." Then he broke down and cried and prayed to His Savior in deep repentance. It is inevitable that true repentance always comes with brokenness of heart. A person must realize the sinfulness of their sin before they repent. Many times we sorrow for sin because of its results but few repent of the sin. Repentance implies not only the acknowledgement of sin, but the forsaking of it as well.

When Simba realizes his sinfulness, he turns around

and goes back to the land of his fathers in order to take his proper place. When King Nebuchadnezzar realized his sin, he praised the God of heaven and was restored to his position. When the prodigal son came to his senses, he returned to his father, made confession, and his father restored him to his rightful place. God forbid that you and I can realize our sin and still remain at the same place. Jesus came to save us out of sin and not in it. It is proper that we first realize that we are lost and come to our senses, leave our old sinful ways and pray to the God of heaven. "If we confess our sins, He is faithful and just to forgive us our sins, and to cleanse us from all unrighteousness" (1 John 1:9). In fact I heard in a Negro spiritual that He's been "listening all the night long, been listening all the night long, been listening all the night long, to hear some sinner pray." So why not pray to Him right now, He's waiting for you as if there were no on else in the world to listen to but you.

CHAPTER 12

"REMEMBER YOU'RE MY SON"

In the middle of Simba's agonizing over the right decision to make, there comes Rafiki, a former aide to his father, the man who anointed Simba at his birthday ceremony. The two get into a conversation that looks silly because Rafiki is so excited about finding the "Messiah." The question, "Who are you?" turns out to be a mountain of a question. The context determines how a person answers that age-old question. Human beings are imbued with the question of their origin, morality and destiny. This is Simba's time. At this time he is battling in his mind about whether he should go back home and save his people and risk his own life or stay in the land of Pumba and Timon where life is rosy.

Admittedly, the land of "Hakuna Matata" is very beautiful. It is really a paradise. In fact as one watches Nala urging Simba to leave that place while walking besides the beautiful falls, a thought comes to mind, "but why would he leave such a beautiful place to go to a land where the hyenas have impoverished the people and destroyed all the glory there was in Pride Lands?" Besides, Simba has grown out of touch with his people now. Is there any need to bother?

But Rafiki, now in his old age, has always longed to see the day when the land would be restored again to its proper state and that has to be done by one of true royal blood, a true son of Mufasa. We can run away from God for a time, but God will always follow us in order to help rebuild His kingdom that has been marred by the scars of sin. The purpose of God's children is to glorify God and get ready for His second coming. And when we are born, we are born into the grand family of God. However, the devil is still alive and his will is that we be alienated from God and His will forever. He fools us into believing a lie. And, over the six thousand years that this world has been in existence, the devil has had enormous experience fooling God's people.

Many times, he uses fear as his weapon, because fear and faith do not share the same room. He threatens to destroy our seemingly good way of life should we follow God's ways. He also threatens us with the fear of loss of the family members, friends and the things that this world has to offer. Thus, many succumb to the devil's threats. But we should not fear any of the devil's threats, because the devil was defeated on Calvary and faith overcame fear.

This reminds me of a story about one time when there was a war between two factions. One side was defeated after heavy fighting between the parties. Then, one of the generals took one of the men at gunpoint forcing him to do all the nasty things that a man can imagine. He was commanded to clean the general's shoes, to take all his clothes off and to climb a tree up and down many times and he did. The general then found human feces and commanded the man to eat it. The man looked at the feces and he looked at the general; the gun was still pointed at him. But the man had made his mind up. He would not eat human feces under any circumstances. He chose that he would rather die than eat that stuff. Only when he had refused the unthinkable did he realize the gun had no bullets. He had done all the stupid things at gunpoint only to realize there were no bullets.

Many of us are afraid of the devil because he threatens us with loss of this and that and even the loss of life, but let the word be heard that the devil's gun has no bullets. If he kills this flesh, he has not destroyed you because at the resurrection, you will be rewarded with eternal life, but his reward is death.

Let us not be afraid of coming to God because of the devil's threats. Rafiki takes Simba to a simple intellectual practical school. The Father himself speaks to Simba, urging him to remember who he is, the one true king. Like Mufasa's conversation with his son, when we forget who we are, we forget God too. In this instance, however, We should not forget that the devils power was not taken away from him, thus he can still perform these kind of miracles to deceive many. We can still deduce a lesson from this tale however. It is important for us not to forget who we are and therefore that fundamental thing will remind us who God is. God talks to us through the Bible and informs us that we are His children and that He loves us with a great love. We are a royal priesthood, a holy nation (1 Peter 2:8, 9).

Jonah tried to run away from the will of God but God in His love followed him. Jonah was sent to warn the people of Niniveh about the impending penalty of their sin but he chose to run away to go to Tarshish instead. On the way, God brought winds to the sea and the boat that Jonah was on threatened to collapse. The crew threw many goods into the sea to make the boat lighter but that did not help. It was not until Jonah offered himself to be thrown into the sea that the water grew calm. A whale swallowed him and he was in there three days and three nights. The Bible says Jonah prayed while in the belly of the whale and the whale spat him on the beach near Niniveh.

The message was clear to Jonah, "remember you are my son."

CHAPTER 13

RAFIKI THE WITCH

Rafiki is a dear character in the tale of Pride Lands. Without him, many of the scenes would have been difficult to enjoin. Rafiki is the "spiritual" guru of the tribe and he comes to anoint baby Simba at his celebrations. The name Rafiki means friend in the Kiswahili language. He is the embodiment of the circle of life, anointing one king after the other and their sons as long as he lives. He carries with him a stick with two pockets attached to it. In those pockets are some valuable possessions that Rafiki uses for divination and to cast lots.

At his home, he has the image of Simba drawn on a tree. It is a glimmer of hope for the Pride Lands that when the Father passes, Simba will take over. But when the developments of Scar and the killing of King Mufasa follow, Simba runs away and the tribe thinks he's dead. In that vein, the glimmer of hope disappears as Scar takes over the throne and gives it to the hyenas. Rafiki, in despair, rubs off the image of Simba from the tree because hope has disappeared.

After many years when there is now a famine in the land, Simba and his friends Pumba and Timon are relaxing outside and Simba withdraws from them to go sit on his own. As he sits down, the dust and firs that come from him are taken by the wind right back to Pride Lands and Rafiki grabs a hold of them. After performing a rite, he deciphers Simba is alive; he follows it up and it is proven.

The spirit mediums have always been there from the time of old and they are still here today, some even claiming to be Christian spiritualists. The Bible does not leave us to guess about these and their "spiritual" phenomenon. The basis of spiritualism is the first lie that "you shall not surely die" (Genesis 3:4). Knowing this, God put many warnings for His children against spiritualism. It is the greatest deception there is and the greatest there is going to be. The devil and his angels are just using it as a means of communicating their deception (Rev 12:4, 9) to God's people.

In Leviticus 19:31, God says "Give no regard to mediums and familiar spirits; do not seek after them, to be defiled by them: I am the Lord your God." NKJV Deuteronomy 18:10,11 is even more clear, "There shall not be found among you anyone who makes his son or his daughter pass through the fire, or one who practices witchcraft, or a soothsayer, or one who interprets omens, or a sorcerer, or one who conjures spells, or a medium, or a spiritist, or one who calls up the dead." NKJV The prophet Isaiah thinks it's foolishness, "and when they say to you, 'seek those who are mediums and wizards, who whisper and mutter,' should not a people seek their God? Should they seek the dead on behalf of the living? To the law and to the testimony! If they do not speak according to this word, it is because there is no light in them." (Isaiah 8:20) NKJV And here's another chilling, but firm warning, "But the cowardly, the unbelieving, the vile, the murderers, the sexually immoral, those who practice magic arts, the idolaters and all liars— their place will be in the fiery lake of burning sulphur. This is the second death." (Revelation 21:8) NIV

The danger of spiritualism is that it is very deceptive. One author couldn't have put it better, "while it formerly denounced Christ and the Bible, it now professes to accept both. But the Bible is interpreted in a manner that is pleasing to the un-renewed heart, while its solemn and vital truths are made of no effect. Love is dwelt upon as the chief attribute of God, but it is degraded to a weak sentimentalism, making little distinction between good and evil. God's justice, His denunciations of sin, the requirements of His holy law, are all kept out of sight. The people are taught to regard the Decalogue as a dead letter. Pleasing, bewitching fables captivate the senses and lead men to reject the Bible as the foundation of their faith. Christ is as verily denied as before; but Satan has so blinded the eyes of the people that the deception is not discerned."(Great Controversy p.558)

One of the reasons spiritualism is so deceptive to many is that it is often practiced in church and by ministers, and many who are sick are healed. In fact, the Bible predicts that in the last days, the devil will unleash great signs and miracles in a final effort to masterfully deceive as many as he possibly can. John the Revelator saw it as "three unclean spirits like frogs" (Rev 16:13). Revelation 13:13, 14 states, "He performs great signs, so that he even makes fire come down from heaven on the earth in the sight of men. And he deceives those who dwell on the earth by those signs which he was granted to do." NKJV

Because this phenomenon is found almost everywhere people are, it has become a part of them, thus the devil is gaining more and more adherence to his deception because he has been able to use spiritualism in movies and television shows such as "Touched by an Angel," "Left Behind," The Vampire Slayer," "The Witch" and the like.

The scene when King Mufasa speaks to Simba is dramatic and it is one of the many examples where many can easily be caught unawares by a very nice movie or program. Rafiki works his magic as usual and the "spirit" of Mufasa comes back to remind his son to stand up to his title. Stemming out of spiritualism, this important scene cannot go without scrutiny because this is a pivotal point in the salvation of many.

This scene has some truth, such as "He lives in you," pointing to the circle of life. Anybody would have the blood of their father flowing in their veins. But that truth is mixed with error, such as that the dead King Mufasa talks to Simba. Unsuspecting people can take this very lightly, but the fact is true, the devil is preparing the people for the greatest delusion there will ever be in the history of this world. Thus, by watching that scene, he wants the very impressionable kids and their parents to believe that the dead are watching over us and they can still speak to us given the right circumstances. Taking this point lightly has led many to believe in the lie that was told by the serpent at the scene of the first sin, and such will not be able to stand the delusion.

As a follower of Jesus Christ, it is very important for one to always stay in touch with heaven through prayer as it is important to breathe, and heaven will help put spiritual spectacles on the things we watch, hear, or think. That way the delusion that is coming to sweep most of the world will not find us inattentive. I guess one could go and tell Rafiki, that if he likes spiritual things, it is a noble desire; the Lord is still welcoming preachers of the gospel truth as found in Jesus Christ. I'm sure Pride Lands would be delighted to hear about the free saving power of Jesus Christ.

CHAPTER 14

ARMAGEDDON IN PRIDE LANDS

When Simba finally makes the firm decision to leave the land of Hakuna Matata, he's not delayed by anything. Even Rafiki the preacher cannot stop him. Strolling back home to take his proper place in the circle of life, he must have thought, "I'll go back to my people, and whatever my past may be, I'll have to face it when I get there." But it's not going to be easy. King Scar is not going to relinquish power without a fight. So he must face his uncle squarely and fight him. It is an anticipated battle just like the much talked about battle of Armageddon found in Revelation 16.

Much has been published in many circles about the battle of Armageddon, books have been written, sermons preached, and even movies made, but a careful Bible student will discover that Armageddon is not a physical war more than it is a spiritual battle, the last battle between good and evil. The book of Revelation, where the story of Armageddon is written, is a symbolic book. It forms a lot of imagery mainly borrowed from the stories and enactments of the Old Testament. For example, in Revelation 1:12 John turns to see the voice that was speaking to him and he sees seven golden lamp stands. These are the same as those found in Exodus 25:37. Revelation 11:8 says, "and their dead bodies will lie in the street of the great city which mystically is called Sodom and Egypt, where also their Lord was crucified." Obviously, this is symbolic language with overtones of Old Testament imagery. One has to go back, read the related Old Testament stories, and come up with the meaning.

Revelation 16:16 reads, "And they gathered them together to the place which in Hebrew is called Armageddon." Popular interpretations equate this to a real place in Israel where the final great battle of earth will take place. The best interpretation will come from understanding the meaning of this biblical term

"Armageddon." The term appears only once in the Bible and the Bible gives us a clue. It is called Armageddon in the Hebrew tongue. Hebrew is one of the languages of the Old Testament. Thus, we have to find its meaning in the Hebrew tongue.

A breakdown of the word Armageddon will help provide an interpretation. "Har" means hill or mountain. Thus, the word means mountain of "meggido." However, there is no mountain of Meggido, nor has there been one anywhere on earth, but there is a valley of Meggido, a city of Meggido and a plain of Meggido. Thus, we now have to find its symbolic meaning.

The plain of Meggido has been an important strategic place in Israel. The most famous and decisive battles of Israel were fought around the area. At Meggido, Barak and Deborah defeated Sisera and his army (Judges 5:19-21), there Ahaziah was shot by Jehu (2 Kings 9:27), and at the same place Josiah was killed by Pharoah Neco (2 Kings 23-29; Zechariah 12:11). Mount Carmel rises above the plain of Meggido and it happens to be the famous place of Elijah's battle with the prophets of Baal. The spiritual meaning of the Old Testament battle carries on to the New.

In the days of the prophet Elijah, Ahab the king of Israel had led the children of Israel into Baal worship as a result of the influence of Jezebel his idolatrous wife, and that did not please God. Elijah therefore made a daring offer for a contest to find out who is the true God. "How long halt ye between two opinions?" He asked, "If the LORD be God, follow him: but if Baal, follow him" (1 Kings 18:21). In a showdown that only bold children of God can do, Elijah gathered Israel on top of Mount Carmel. He then decided the true God would be the One who sends fire on to the altar of their prophet. The prophets of Baal made their altars ready and ran around them all morning and even all day. There was no fire that came. Elijah mocked them to "cry aloud" lest he (Baal) be sleeping or on a trip. They shouted loud and cut themselves with knives until blood gushed out on them. After the time of the evening sacrifice, there was no fire from Baal.

Then Elijah gathered and called all of them to come nearer. He then took twelve stones according to the number of the tribes of Israel then made an altar to the Lord. Elijah then dug a trench of water around the altar and ordered them to pour water on the altar with the wood.

> *And it came to pass at the time of the offering of the evening sacrifice, that Elijah the prophet came near, and said, LORD God of Abraham, Isaac, and of Israel, let it be known this day that thou art God in Israel, and that I am thy servant, and that I have done all these things at thy word.*
>
> *Hear me, O LORD, hear me, that this people may know that thou art the LORD God, and that thou hast turned their heart back again.*
>
> *Then the fire of the LORD fell, and consumed the burnt sacrifice, and the wood, and the stones, and the dust, and licked up the water that was in the trench.*
>
> *And when all the people saw it, they fell on their faces: and they said, The LORD, he is the God; the LORD, he is the God.* (1 Kings 18:36-39)

Thus, Mount Carmel since that day has epitomized the great success in favor of the true God of heaven.

John the Revelator remembers the scene and finds its spiritual meaning to fall within the sixth of a series of seven last plagues of Revelation. Like the battle of Elijah on Mount Carmel, the last day battle will be fought at Armageddon. However, the latter is a spiritual battle and not a physical one. The devil will bring his mastermind of deception by performing miracles and pretending to be the Christ, yet in contradiction to the Biblical teachings. The majority of the people will believe a lie which comes as a strong over-mastering delusion (2 Thessalonians 2:9-12). This great delusion will also be forced on to the majority of the people of the world. The two beasts of Revelation 13 will make an alliance, with the second beast, a political power that forces the people to worship the first beast which is a religious power.

The hardest and the greatest of wars will be Armageddon. It will not be about missiles and scuds, and tankers, but it will be a battle for the hearts and minds of the people. Like Elijah's battle on Mount Carmel, Armageddon's battle will involve worship. Again, the question will be asked, "How long halt ye between two opinions? If the LORD be God, follow him: but if Baal, [then] follow him" (1 Kings 18:21). This will be the climax of the ages. People all over the world must choose their allegiance, whether it be God or Baal (the beasts). This will be the last chance for the devil's attempt to destroy God's people, thus he will be the instigator of the war.

Masterful though the deceptions will be for the majority of the people, the faithful few will stand on the side of the Lord. The final word must be said. Who is God? Who must be worshipped? God will not keep silent. Daniel saw it coming and he records it vividly. "And at that time shall Michael stand up, the great prince which standeth for the children of thy people: and there shall be a time of trouble, such as never was since there was a nation even to that same time: and at that time thy people shall be delivered, every one that shall be found written in the book. And many of them that sleep in the dust of the earth shall awake, some to everlasting life, and some to shame and everlasting contempt."(Daniel 12:1,2).

In the context of the preparation of the battle of Armageddon, as John puts forward the portrayal of the battle, he does not forget to give us warning, "Behold, I am coming as a thief. Blessed is the one who watches and keeps his garments so that he does not walk naked and they see his shame." (Rev 16:15) NKJV When Simba fights his final battle with his uncle Scar, he almost looks like he's going to fail the test. Scar seems to triumph in the battle when he splashes fire on Simba's face causing him to almost plunge into the burning fire, or so it looks. Apparently, Simba is more powerful than his older uncle. He catapults himself from the seeming Gehenna and ends up on the vantage ground. Even though it looks like he's going to lose, he won't. Thus the assurance is given to God's people, that no matter how tense the situation may be, no matter how hard and daunting the situation, Jesus will finally come in the end to take His place and redeem His faithful few to the uttermost. The devil may look like he's on the winning side because the media seems to portray that, but not so. As the Lord liveth, He will not keep silent on our matter. Our duty is to keep our guard and watch.

The battle of Armageddon will surely come and it will be very soon, but not in the way that most Christians interpret it to be. It will not be a physical war by the powers of this world some place in Palestine, it will be in the hearts and minds of the people. It will not be an easy battle to be involved in. The mastermind of deception will draw many to his side with false worship. Only those that make the choice to follow Jesus will be able to stand for He will help them stand the test. Have you made your choice today? Our tomorrow is dependent on the choices we make today. If you are reading this, it's not yet too late. I would strongly urge you to choose Jesus; He's on the winning side.

CHAPTER 15

SIMBA

The name Simba is very interesting, not only because that's my name but also because of its import and significance. Depending on where one comes from in Africa, the name Simba has different meanings. If one is in Zimbabwe, my home country, it means strength or power. It is a popular name for Shona boys in Zimbabwe. My full name is Simbarashe which is a Shona word meaning the power of God. The short version is Simba. In East Africa, it means lion in the Kiswahili language. However, when one is in South Africa it is the name of a brand of potato chips, named after "Simba the Lion" (Kisawahili) in honor of Leon Greyvenstein who founded the idea of Simba chips back in 1956 in that country. Simba is also a popular brand of beer manufactured by Brasseries du Lion in the Democratic Republic of the Congo. The latter two get their meaning from the Kiswahili meaning of lion. The two languages, Shona and Kiswahili are Bantu languages, which constitute a grouping belonging to the Niger-Congo family. These are languages spoken basically east and south of Nigeria; i.e., central Africa, east Africa, and southern Africa. These languages have a number of similarities in meaning. One would argue that Simba, meaning strength in Shona is intrinsically related to the fact that the lion is the strongest animal in the jungle.

As one watches the last scene of the "Lion King," it is inevitable that Simba is not only the endeared one as compared to his uncle Scar, but he emerges as the braver and more humane. After the discourse that appears to be the judgment, hyenas and Mufasa's family are watching, Scar tells them that Simba was responsible for his father's death and, wanting to kill Simba, he pins him down and Simba dangerously hangs on the edge of Pride Rock's promontory. This brings Scar's memories back to the day he killed his father and he says, "This looks familiar." Thinking that he has won the battle, Scar tells

the truth, and that enrages Simba who leaps up and pins
Scar down to the ground, forcing him to reveal more of
the truth. In that moment, one would think Simba would
want to cut Scar's throat right away, but instead, he tells
him to "run and not come back." However, Scar, scared
of that proposal, still wants to kill Simba and the battle
ends with him going down to sheol. Simba wins the battle
and takes his rightful place in the circle of life.

The character of Simba in the last scene of this popular
movie goes along with its biblical namesake of Revelation.
In chapter 5, we are told of a scene when John saw a book
written on the inside and on the back and sealed with seven
seals. Then a strong angel proclaimed, "Who is worthy
to open the scroll and to loose its seals?" And no one in
heaven or on the earth or under the earth was able to open
the scroll, or to look at it." (Revelation 5:2, 3) NKJV Then
John began to weep. "But one of the elders said to me, "Do
not weep. Behold, the Lion (Simba) of the tribe of Judah,
the Root of David, has prevailed to open the scroll and to
loose its seven seals." (Revelation 5:5) NKJV

In one of the most interesting passages of the Bible,
we see a repetition of one of Revelation's motifs – the
thought of what one hears and the reality of what one
ends up seeing. In Revelation, a few times the hearer
hears one thing but when they turn to see, they behold
another. In Revelation 1:10 John heard a voice like the
voice of a trumpet, "and I turned to see the voice that
was speaking with me. And having turned I saw seven
golden lampstands." (NASB) Revelation 7:4 resonates
with chapter 1. "And I heard the number of those who
were sealed, one hundred and forty-four thousand sealed
from every tribe of the sons of Israel." "After these things
I looked, and behold, a great multitude, which no one
could count, from every nation and all tribes and peoples
and tongues, standing before the throne and before the
Lamb, clothed in white robes, and palm branches were
in their hands."(verse 9, NASB)

In Revelation 5, John hears about "the lion of the tribe
of Judah" that overcame. The lion symbolizes greatness,
and it connotes power, two phenomena that the devil

uses as a ploy to lure many to his side. Everyone wishes to be great and everyone yearns for some power in order to feel important. The reason there is a lot of commotion in the world today can be traced to these two. The major ingredient used to attain power is money and yet the apostle said, "The love of money is the root of all evil...." (1 Timothy 6:10). No wonder people go to lengths in their pursuit of power and greatness. A great many have lost their lives due to this. Governments have been built and destroyed in the pursuit of power and money. Homes have been broken, and divorces filed as a result of each partner wanting to take rulership of the home. The love of power and greatness is the source of the world's greatest maladies. The ills of today's societies include hatred, envy, jealousy, resentment, and many more.

The fact that Jesus is equated to a lion gives us a glimpse into His ways of doing things. After John hears about the lion of the tribe of Judah, he turns around to see, and behold he did not see a lion, but he saw a lamb "as if it had been slain." Jesus is the greatest being and all power resides in Him for He created the heavens and the earth. He made everything there is, and thus 2000 years ago when on a ship with His disciples one day, He went into an inner room and slept, and the winds and the waves threatened to destroy the ship and its inhabitants. Having been awakened by His scared disciples, He stood and simply said, "Peace, be still." And the wind ceased, and there was a great calm (Mark 4:39). While in His hometown, as he taught in one house, was brought to Him a paralytic. When He saw the faith in the four men who had dropped him through the roof, Jesus said, "Your sins are forgiven." When the Pharisees in the room thought in their hearts that He blasphemed, He answered the unspoken query and said, "Why do you think evil in your hearts? For which is easier, to say, "Your sins are forgiven you,' or to say, 'Arise and walk'? But that you may know that the Son of Man has *power* on earth to forgive sins"— then He said to the paralytic, "Arise, take up your bed, and go to your house." And he arose and departed to his house. Now when the multitudes saw it, they marveled

and glorified God, who had given such **power** to men."
(Matthew 9:1-5; NKJV, emphasis mine)

There is no doubt that Jesus had the ultimate power to do anything for others. The lesson that humanity needs to learn from the story of Revelation 5 is that when we **hear** of the great power of Jesus, it is then imperative that we turn and **look** at how He achieves it – in humility, like a lamb. John turned to see and behold the lion he had heard looked like a lamb.

While in the US, I used to work in a nursing home in Indiana, just across the state border from Michigan, in order to support my education while in graduate school. One day as I helped one of the old women while she lay on her bed, without any warning and all of a sudden, I got a very big blow from her in my right eye. In shock, I did not know what to do, but of course, I saw stars. For no apparent reason my eye was shattered by a woman I was helping. Now, in a normal case, the tendency would be to hit the old woman back, but no, I would not do that. The laws of the land did not permit that. That would be elderly abuse. But when I look at it, I wonder who was really abused. Since that time, my right eye has been much redder than the other one.

When working with the elderly, the United States government gives a set of rules to protect the rights of the elderly. Should one not follow these rules and infringe on the rights of the elderly or disabled, they could not only go to prison for a long time, but they will never be allowed to work with such people again. As I evaluated these rules, I thought all those that work with the elderly and the disabled ought to be better Christians, simply because the same rights that they ascribe to this group of people and are followed religiously are the same basic rights that Christianity gives to the world. Much as we must not return the favor of a beating or verbal abuse to a client, we should not do that to anyone else, not because we are afraid of being fired, but because the blood of Jesus has so much changed our lives that we view the abuse as a blessing to us. Jesus said in unequivocal terms, "Blessed are they which are persecuted for righteousness' sake: for theirs is the kingdom of heaven." (Matthew 5:10)

Even though in my case, I would not have hit the old woman who shattered my eye, regardless of the rules, it is only true humility that can keep us from the need for revenge. That kind of humility can only be found in the life of Jesus Christ our perfect example. As we focus our eyes on Jesus then we begin to see the difference in how He treated people and how He was treated and since we are Christians, the followers of Jesus He will give us the power to endure the temptations which by ourselves we would not be able to. It is not an easy road, but Jesus has already traveled through it on our behalf so if we only abide in Him then He will do it through us. And only then can we gain true greatness.

When the Sanhedrin condemned Jesus to die the death of the cross, there was no justification for the death penalty, except that the Jewish leaders were troubled about this Man who was taking away their influence and power. And Jesus did not protest for His rights; instead, He went as a lamb to the slaughter and He never said a mumbling word. (Isiaah 53:7) He hung on the cross and died for the sins of the world. While on the cross, He said, "It is finished" (John 19:30), to mean that His mission of dying for the sinful world had been accomplished. As a result, Paul in Acts says, there's no other name we can be saved by except the name of Jesus (Acts 4:12).

What a contrast with the way the devil would rather have us think. This is portrayed in the world's political system today where it is a dog eat dog situation of the survival of the fittest. Movies that show a revengeful spirit are also very popular and the devil has made quite some inroads with that kind of thinking. However, the warrior spirit is far from the way God would have us live. Humility is the key, no wonder the lesson of Jesus, if one strikes you on one cheek, give them another. (Matthew 5: 39) During the passion night when Peter striked the ear of the high priest's servant, Jesus said, "Put your sword in its place for all who take the sword will perish by the sword." (Matthew 26: 51,52; John 18:10,11) NKJV And Paul alludes, "That is why, for Christ's sake, I delight in weaknesses, in insults, in hardships, in persecutions, in difficulties. For when I am weak, then I am strong." (2 Corinthians 12:10) NIV What a contrast this thought is with popular sentiment. The power of an individual does not consist of the things they may possess, nor is it derived from the position they may hold. Real power is found in humility as Jesus showed.

While no selfish person will be imbued with the power of Jesus, true humility on the other hand will be rewarded both in this life and in the life to come. Humility consists of trusting in Jesus in all our daily endeavors and telling the truth in love. As long as we humble ourselves, and pray and have faith as little as a mastered seed, Jesus said, we could move mountains and live a life of peace and joy in the Lord. And in a little while, the greater reward will come when Jesus comes back again to take us home to live with Him.

CHAPTER 16

PRIDE LANDS RESTORED

After the fierce battle of Armageddon, where Simba takes the risk of failure, he triumphs in the end. Now it is his duty as the son of the king to take his place in Pride Lands and restore the land to normalcy. Simba does take his place and marries the love of his life, Nala, in a captivating story that seems to end with the famous, "And, they lived happily ever after." They are blessed with a little baby and the circle of life keeps rolling as this time, the son of a king has a little baby too, but just that it is in the land restored to its original state before Scar marred it with the hyenas. Now as in the very first scene of the "Lion King" the last scene is glorious, having all the animal kingdom come to give homage and celebrate and welcome the new king's firstborn.

The writer of the "Lion King" seems to have been inspired in biblical connotations. Just like the first scene and the last scene in the story, the first and the last scenes of the Bible are glorious. The first two chapters of Genesis are glorious, beginning with the newly created earth, climaxing in the creation of the first parents. Adam and Eve were placed in the Garden of Eden, then God rested on the Sabbath day and hallowed it and made it holy. In the movie, all is well until uncle Scar appears. In the Bible, all is well too, until the scene when the serpent the devil comes into the picture. As soon as he is introduced, the devil comes in and mars the good picture there was in the Garden of Eden, bringing sin into the world. Sixty six books later, in the last two chapters, earth and heaven are restored. What a marvelous picture. In addition, the King's son, Jesus Christ is King of the new heaven and the new earth. Sin has been eradicated. Death has also died. Revelation 20:14 records, "And death and Hades were thrown into the lake of fire." Paul agrees, "The last enemy that will be abolished is death." (1 Corinthians 15:26) Uncle Scar, the devil who taunted the people of

God is no more for "...the devil that deceived them was thrown into the lake of fire and brimstone, where the beast and the false prophet are also. . ." (Rev 20:10).

The Bible does not leave us to guess about what will happen to God's children after all the warfare of the great controversy is finished. He said to his disciples before he left, "Let not your heart be troubled: ye believe in God, believe also in me. In my Father's house are many mansions: if it were not so, I would have told you. I go to prepare a place for you. And if I go and prepare a place for you, I will come again, and receive you unto myself; that where I am, there ye may be also." (John 14:1-3) Jesus has promised a place for us, all we need is to accept Him by faith, and all shall be ours. Paul helps us to put things into perspective. The place that God is preparing for His children is far beyond human comprehension. No matter how much we can stretch our imaginations, we will not be able to comprehend the magnitude of the beauty of heaven. "But as it is written, eye hath not seen, nor ear heard, neither have entered into the heart of man, the things which God hath prepared for them that love him" (1 Corinthians 2:9).

John puts the word picture very clearly, "And I saw a new heaven and a new earth: for the first heaven and the first earth were passed away; and there was no more sea. And I John saw the holy city, New Jerusalem, coming down from God out of heaven, prepared as a bride adorned for her husband."(Rev 21:1, 2) New Jerusalem is its name. Jerusalem means "city of peace", and it will be far different from the Jerusalem found in the land of Israel today. In the New Jerusalem, there will be no death, there will be no disease, there will be no sorrow. All things shall have been made new. Heaven will be glorious. John was quick to mention that there was no longer any sea. This was a means of separation for him on the Isle of Patmos and the rest of the free world. John is relieved therefore, to notice that in the New Jerusalem, there was no more sea. The city that John saw "had a great and high wall, with twelve gates, and at the gates twelve angels; and names were written on them, which are those of the twelve tribes of the sons of Israel. There were three gates on the east and three gates on the north and three gates on the south and three gates on the west" (Rev 21: 12, 13) NASB

The names of the children of Jacob that make the twelve tribes encompass many different characteristics. Given the characters of the children of Jacob, it gives assurance that anyone can be saved. It further shows us that heaven will be full of sinners who are forgiven. The twelve sons had characters that left much to be desired. A list of the sins of these twelve would include murderers, liars, and adulterers. If these not so perfect descendants of Jacob will have their names written on the gates of the walls of the New Jerusalem, then I have a chance. The choice is mine. That thought helps make the good news even better. Salvation came to us as a free gift for all, but soon that door will be closed.

As one reads the dimensions and measurements of the city that John saw, (the city built four square, the walls of jasper, the city pure gold, the foundation stones adorned with every kind of precious stone, and the gates made of pearl), it's not about the city but *who* will be in the city – Jesus Christ Son of the living God. If Jesus were not there, it would be like going for a wedding and finding no bridegroom there. The cry of every child of God will be to see Jesus, the One who died for us. It is said that the city had no sun nor moon for its lamp was the Lamb.

In the middle of the city will flow a river, the river of the water of life coming out from the throne of God and of the Lamb, and on either side of the river is the tree of life, bearing twelve kinds of fruit, yielding its fruit every month and the leaves of the tree are for the healing of the nations. (Rev 22:1, 2) In the middle of the garden of Eden was the tree of life, and in the middle of the New Jerusalem will be the tree of life. Humanity, since sin entered the world, has suffered a degeneration of stature. The leaves of the tree of life will be for the healing of the nations. When we shall eat of the tree of life, we shall be rejuvenated to grow again to the stature that God originally planned for us to have. What a day that will be! I can imagine the long table where the children of

God will sit on the welcoming day. I can only imagine how grand and beautiful the angelic choir's music will be. One other thing to look forward to is to hear God Himself sing. I also look forward to the heavenly Sabbath worship day as Isaiah saw it. (Isaiah 66:23).

The thought of heaven only brings tears of joy upon its contemplation. One can only imagine the kind of song that will come from the voices of the redeemed. When all of God's singers get home, what a day that will be. The songwriter says,

"Sing the wondrous love of Jesus, sing His mercy and His grace.

In the mansions bright and blessed, He'll prepare for us a place.

When we all get to heaven, what a day of rejoicing that will be!

When we all see Jesus, we'll sing and shout the victory."
—Mrs. J. H. Wilson

Then, and only then, will we begin to see that the troubles we would have sustained on this earth will be by far outweighed by the glory that Jesus will provide. Today, when temptation comes our way, let us endure the trial, no matter how hard, because that temptation is not worth to compare with the glories that Jesus is preparing for His children. I would like to make it to the kingdom because there I will not only see my loved ones who have passed away, but I will see Jesus. Don't you want to join the throng that will make up that band? Remember, it's free of charge. Only accept the grace offered through Jesus Christ our Savior. Even Pride Lands restored cannot compare with the real Land of the Saved.

We'd love to have you download our catalog of titles we publish at:

www.TEACHServices.com

or write or email us your thoughts, reactions, or criticism about this or any other book we publish at:

TEACH Services, Inc.
254 Donovan Road
Brushton, NY 12916

info@TEACHServices.com

or you may call us at:

518/358-3494

Breinigsville, PA USA
15 February 2010
232514BV00004B/4/P

Simba (780)722 2926 www.gospelinthelionking.com